Handbook Of Data Reliability Engineering

OrangeBooks Publication

1st Floor, Rajhans Arcade, Mall Road, Kohka, Bhilai, Chhattisgarh 490020

Website: **www.orangebooks.in**

© Copyright, 2024, Author

All rights reserved. No part of this book may be reproduced, stored in a retrieval system, or transmitted, in any form by any means, electronic, mechanical, magnetic, optical, chemical, manual, photocopying, recording or otherwise, without the prior written consent of its writer.

First Edition, 2024
ISBN: 978-93-5621-863-5

HANDBOOK OF
DATA RELIABILITY ENGINEERING

A COMPREHENSIVE GUIDE TO MANAGE RELIABILITY IN DATA ORGANIZATIONS

RAJDEEP MANDAL

OrangeBooks Publication
www.orangebooks.in

A Comprehensive Guide To Manage Reliability In Data Organizations

Rajdeep Mandal

Introduction

We are familiar with the time-tested SRE principles coined by Google, which effectively manage web and mobile applications. DRE adopts the same philosophy for data workloads. DRE principles focus primarily on post-production observability methodologies. To address observability, monitoring, performance, efficiency, and cost optimization, the DRE framework is thoroughly explored and explained in this book, ensuring reliable data solutions.

However, achieving the data reliability North Star—ensuring reduced data downtime and meeting data quality metrics such as accuracy, freshness, and latency—is crucial. The challenge lies in improving observability in complex data solutions where over a thousand pipelines run 24/7, adhering to the SRE handrails set by Google.

This book offers clear guidance from three perspectives: People, Process, and Technology. While most SRE books emphasize the technological aspect, it's essential to align people and processes carefully with the technical vision or the North Star of your data organization. Otherwise, everything remains theoretical.

In essence, this book delves into end-to-end approaches to Data Reliability Engineering. Considering it as the first published book on this topic wouldn't be an overstatement. It will assist you in crafting your strategy and achievable roadmap for establishing data reliability.

Thank you for selecting this book. I am confident it will provide you with the answers you've been seeking but haven't yet found collated and documented.

Content

Introduction v

PART - 1
SRE & DRE

Chapter One
SRE Principles and Practices in Data
Organizations 3

Chapter Two
DRE Introduction 7

PART - 2
How to Set Up Data Reliability Engineering

Chapter Three
DRE - People 12

Chapter Four
DRE – Process 17

Chapter Five
DRE - Technology 20

FinOps 40

Bibliography 56

Acknowledgement 58

SRE & DRE

Let's enumerate the SRE principles. Please note that in this chapter, we will focus solely on those SRE principles and practices applicable to data organizations. Subsequently, we will incorporate additional principles essential for addressing challenges unique to data organizations. As we delve into all the principles and practices within data organizations, the practical roadmap will be denoted as the DRE framework. Please consult the Venn diagram below to grasp the relationship between SRE and DRE.

In simple terms, DRE is a subset of SRE, accompanied by its own attributes aimed at tackling challenges within data organizations. For references to SRE books published by Google, a link is provided in the bibliography section of this book.

SRE Principles
Embracing Risk
Eliminating Toil
Release Engineering
Service Level Objectives

Monitoring Distributed System

SRE Practices
Practical Alerting
Being On-Call
Effective Troubleshooting
Emergency Response
Managing Incidents
Postmortem Culture: Learning from Failure
Tracking Outages
Handling Overload
Reliable Product Launches at Scale

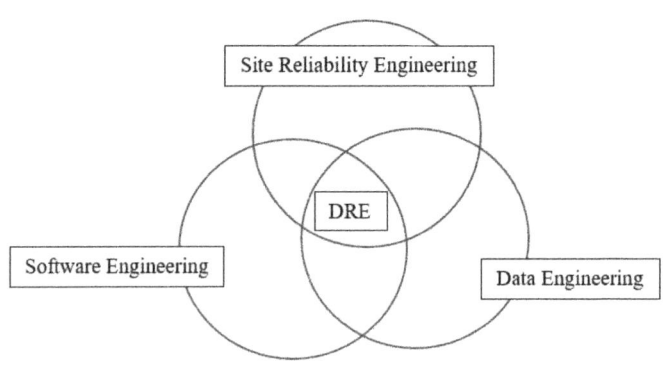

Chapter One
SRE Principles and Practices in Data Organizations

North star for implementing DRE framework will be to achieve following:

1. Availability
2. Monitoring
3. Performance
4. Efficiency
5. Cost Optimization

SRE Principles in the light of DRE

Embracing Risk: It is a mindset that as a DRE, you need to adopt and evangelize as a culture to stakeholders and end users. In data organization, the risk of production environment disruption is quite common. Therefore, it's crucial to relax and focus on the root cause rather than panicking. Maintain control of situations and set clear expectations for end users regarding ETA. Be transparent and assertive in communication, basing decisions on the assessment of the situation and RCA.

Eliminating Toil: This is easier said than done. While we all aspire to automate everything under the sun, it's essential to consider the value addition and cost involved in automation. Automation is particularly beneficial for manual, repetitive, non-value adding clerical tasks, as it helps to reduce toil.

Release Engineering: A stringent change management process should be in place to avoid surprises in automated data workflows.

Service Level Objectives: The availability of data to end users depends on component systems and/or design limitations. Clear expectations should be set with end users regarding report load time, data latency, and/or data freshness.

Monitoring Distributed Systems: This becomes super complex when dealing with data organization. In modern BI solutions, the entire solution is usually not monolithic but based on a microservices architecture. Numerous data handling applications are integrated to deliver the entire workflow.

On the next page, you will learn how to couple SRE practices in the data reliability strategy. However, these are all short-term goals, which will only lay the baseline upon which you will build a long-term strategy to achieve the north stars mentioned at the beginning of this chapter.

SRE Practices:

Practical Alerting: It is essential to have a monitoring and alert mechanism in place for promptly identifying any failures within the data pipeline. All major cloud service providers offer pre-built monitoring services equipped with alert mechanisms tailored for data pipelines.

Being On-Call: Quick response teams or subject matter experts (SMEs) should be ready to join calls promptly to expedite issue resolution. Additionally, implementing KANBAN or Operational Scrum methodologies aids in prioritizing incidents, with product owners aligned with Service Level Objectives (SLOs).

Effective Troubleshooting: While the primary focus is on swiftly restoring the system to Business As Usual (BAU), there is also a need for a broader focus on long-term strategies to prevent recurring incidents stemming from the same cause. Emergency Response – for immediate action and leading to resolution with effective collaboration among all natural teams.

Incident Management: Develop a dashboard for monitoring incidents categorized by ticket aging and reason for failure. Identifying trends among all tickets is crucial to highlighting high-impact focus areas.

Embracing a Postmortem Culture: Learning from Failure – We ought to integrate operational issues with software solutions (LLD, HLD) for sustainable resolutions, rather than resorting to temporary fixes. This necessitates collaboration with the development team and solution architects.

Ensuring Reliable Product Launches at Scale: Implement rigorous change management procedures, preceded by comprehensive impact analysis across the internal and integrated environment of the BI solution.

Based on data stack plan your strategy for SRE/DRE.

1. **Software data stack** – datastores for customer-facing app, microservice, cache/cookies
2. Enterprise data stack – data infra/platforms
3. **Modern data stack** – ETL solutions which contain multiple BI products integrated together, working as one big application, which has ingestion, transformation, storage/staging, modelling, and reporting layers.

Chapter Two
DRE Introduction

Thus far, we have explored the application of SRE principles within data organizations. In this chapter, we will continue to build upon these principles as our foundation, delving deeper into topics specific to data organization. We will focus on managing end-to-end reliability from both a support perspective and an assurance perspective from the business/stakeholders.

In modern cloud-based Business Intelligence (BI) solutions, there exist various layers, typically architected to integrate numerous applications to achieve an end-to-end BI solution. I perceive Data Reliability Engineering (DRE) as the endeavor to ensure the reliability of all components within a business intelligence solution. This encompasses the reliability of the platform, the solution workflow (ETL, staging, publish), and the strategy to achieve end-to-end reliability. This involves structuring teams and processes. When amalgamated, we refer to this comprehensive approach as Data Reliability Engineering.

The objectives of DRE are as follows:

1. **Accuracy:** Ensuring a single version of truth.
2. **Consistency:** Establishing trust in each individual data entity.
3. **Validity:** Ensuring the data platform conforms to organizational standards.
4. **Completeness:** Evaluating the comprehensiveness of the data in terms of volume, measures, and attributes required for informed decision-making.
5. **Freshness:** Determining how quickly data can be obtained from the source system.

Key principles within the DRE vertical include:

1. **Data observability:** This involves monitoring health KPIs (to be detailed in later chapters) on the ETL layer, DWH layer, and reporting layer.
2. **Data governance:** Managing Data Quality (Consistency, Accuracy, Completeness, Auditability, Validity), Data Lineage, User Access Management (UAM), Data Security, and implementing alerts on failure (ETL, DWH, Report performance), as well as maintaining a Data Catalog.
3. **Production report performance:** Implementing self-healing pipelines to ensure storage health, memory, and resource management, and monitoring data refresh success rate.

4. **Data service management:** This entails managing the knowledge base, handling incidents, documentation (including pseudo code and run books), implementing stringent Change Management procedures, clearly documenting cross-team agreements, maintaining regular business and supplier connections, establishing a support model for production, and defining clear RACI (Responsible, Accountable, Consulted, Informed) structures.

5. **FinOps for data:** Conducting operational cost analysis, monitoring resource usage statistics, implementing auto-pause services when not in use, and appropriately sizing backend resources to minimize costs.

How to Set Up Data Reliability Engineering

Step One: To comprehend the solution architecture thoroughly, meticulously peruse the high-level design document crafted by the solution architect. Facilitate a comprehensive knowledge transfer session with the solution architect to gain insights. This endeavor will cultivate a profound understanding of the end-to-end workflow spanning from source systems to the reporting layer, as well as the integrated environment encircling it. Such comprehension stands as an essential prerequisite prior to initiating the planning phase for DRE strategies and associated tasks.

Step Two: Break the architecture in several parts, let's consider Medallion Architecture:

1. **Data Source** – Batch processed, Real Time.
2. **Ingestion Layer** – Data Lake or Delta Lake.
3. **Analytics** – Data is transformed in this layer into bronze, silver, and gold quality.
4. **Staging** – DWH layer
5. **Reporting Layer** – Visualization

Step Three: For each of the layers mentioned above, analyze the pipelines—both master and child—that are responsible for overall orchestration. Create a list of master pipelines that, if monitored, can offer insights into the causes of failures. For instance:

1. Pipeline failure between data source and ingestion layer—most likely due to a data availability issue. Either the batch process failed on the source team's side, or the data didn't arrive due to various other causes.

2. Pipeline failure between the ingestion, analytics, and staging layers—indicative of a data quality issue, either at the schema or data value level.

Monitoring each layer of the BI design is crucial as it provides us with a strategy to permanently address issues. It's possible that all layers are functioning as expected, yet reports are running slowly. In such cases, analyzing the Low-Level Design (LLD) and High-Level Design (HLD), along with exploring query optimization scopes, becomes necessary.

A detailed explanation will be provided in this chapter, where we'll explore technological options such as monitoring and self-healing solutions. Additionally, we'll delve into establishing robust processes around the solution, including contractual agreements. Finally, we'll emphasize the importance of building a team with the right mindset and culture, which leads to quicker and sustainable resolutions to any production problems that may arise.

Chapter Three

DRE – People

In order to deliver, implement, and enable DRE (Data Reliability Engineering), a robust team characterized by a clear purpose and explicit cross-team agreements is imperative. A well-defined RACI (Responsible, Accountable, Consulted, Informed) matrix, coupled with a thorough comprehension of its dynamics, stands as the linchpin for achieving success in this endeavor.

1. **Quick Response Team –**

a. **L1 Team -** The individuals comprising this team should possess a comprehensive understanding of the issues at hand and be adept at documenting production issues in a ticket, capturing key statements such as "reporting environment is down" or "<pipeline name> failed at <time>."

Action Item: It is imperative to train this team to assign tickets to the correct team accurately on the first attempt. This step is critical for expediting resolution times.

b. **L2 Team -** This team consists of moderately experienced technicians who will address the tickets. They primarily handle recurring issues inherent to the BI system that can be swiftly resolved. For instance, if a pipeline fails due to a network issue, a manual re-run could resolve it.

Action Item: This team must be trained to conduct initial Root Cause Analysis (RCA). For instance, if the reporting environment is unusually slow, they should possess sufficient knowledge to determine if it is a network issue, high-throughput queries, or prolonged queries causing the slowdown. Furthermore, they should be capable of providing RCA to the L3 team and promptly escalate to them if they uncover deeper issues necessitating a more thorough examination at the code or architecture level.

c. **L3 Team** - This comprises highly experienced technicians with advanced knowledge of architecture, code, specialized platform knowledge, and technology.

Action Item: It is essential to carefully select individuals for this team and designate Subject Matter Experts (SMEs) for each layer within the Medallion architecture. These SMEs will follow the guidance of the DRE lead in improvement programs. Additionally, they should be trained in business values, adopt a product mindset, and foster a culture of research within the team. As SMEs, with the right mindset, intentions, and motivation, it is highly likely that innovative improvement ideas will originate from this team. They play a pivotal role in delivering Proof of Concepts (PoC) and overseeing production deployments.

2. Periodic Connects –

a. Daily - Operational Scrum (KANBAN)

Participants: L1/L2 team, Business Application Owner/Product Owner, L3 team.

Objective: To prioritize/de-prioritize tickets/incidents with PO/BAO's assistance, crucial for achieving a good CSAT score. For instance, among 100 incidents, only 2 may be critical to current business operations. Through this call, the L2/L3 team redirects focus to these identified critical incidents.

Pre-requisite: A dashboard displaying ticket status, priority, aging, trend, and count is essential. Typically, ticketing tools like ServiceNow and Jira offer basic reporting as an out-of-the-box feature.

b. Weekly - Business Connects

Participants: End users/consumers of outbound data from BI solutions.

Objective: To convey the business value delivered, often lacking in L1/L2/L3 teams, bridging this knowledge gap. For example, while all layers in the BI system may operate without errors, customers may complain about insufficient data volume, duplicate data, or unreadable characters in certain columns. This discussion could initiate new projects/programs for Data Reliability Engineers (DREs) on data quality, source system stability, or contractual agreements with data source teams.

c. **Monthly/Quarterly** - Periodic Connects with Solution Architects

Participants: Solution Architect team, DRE lead, L3, Project Manager, and Product Owner.

Objective: Strategy planning and roadmap development based on current solution performance/health. The DRE, being on the ground, shares observed production issues and identifies possible architectural improvement needs in Low-Level Design (LLD) or High-Level Design (HLD). Redefining Service Level Objectives (SLOs) based on component system limitations is a key focus. For instance, a new business requirement might demand increased data freshness, necessitating a new architectural design.

DRE people leadership key factors:

The DRE lead will function as a unifying force among all natural teams, fostering a blameless post-mortem culture, fostering synchronization, and motivating individuals at levels L1/L2/L3, aiding in their knowledge and career advancement.

The team's culture should be rooted in mutual respect, empathy, ambition, motivation, and a sense of accountability. If any team member errs while executing tasks, the DRE lead ought to delve into how processes/documentation can be enhanced, potentially necessitating better knowledge management.

The DRE lead should shoulder failures and consistently spotlight the team in success narratives. This cultivates a lighter atmosphere among team members, fostering innovation and creativity. The team should be able to address issues with composure, without undue stress over deadlines. It is the DRE lead who will establish accurate delivery expectations to stakeholders and shield the team from external conflicts.

In the subsequent chapter, we will delve into constructing processes around the solution for adherence by individuals.

Chapter Four

DRE – Process

In the preceding chapter, we delved into the intricacies of establishing a cohesive team, focusing on aspects such as team behavior, mindset, and culture. Now, our attention shifts towards delineating a systematic process for the team to adhere to. A process, in essence, embodies the prescribed methodology of operation that all teams, united by a common objective - the reliability of solutions, must follow.

1. **Managing Incidents**: The first step entails creating a dashboard to monitor Incident Key Performance Indicators (KPIs), as suggested by the ITIL framework. These KPIs encompass various metrics such as incident aging, categorization, priority, weekly/monthly trends, and adherence to Service Level Agreements (SLAs). The meticulous tracking and management of these aspects through a centralized dashboard are paramount.

2. **Managing Knowledge**: The second facet revolves around effectively managing troubleshooting runbooks and user access protocols via a comprehensive knowledge base. This repository of knowledge, accessible through articles or a SharePoint site, empowers the L1/L2 team to swiftly

address known issues. The democratization of knowledge forms the cornerstone of promptly restoring the production environment from any disruptions.

3. **Product Documentation**: Next, meticulous documentation of product-related essentials is imperative. This includes the Solution Architect's High-Level Design (SAHLD), transformation logic pseudo code, critical pipeline listings, data catalog, and data lineage. Such documentation must be consistently updated and centralized in platforms like a Knowledge Management portal, or a dedicated SharePoint site tailored for bespoke Business Intelligence solutions.

4. **Stringent Change Management**: A stringent change management protocol is indispensable. This involves conducting detailed impact analyses within the BI solution and integrated environments, devising clear rollback strategies, documenting change tickets with requisite approvals, and formulating comprehensive test strategies. Regular weekly coordination meetings prior to change releases, involving the development team, L1/L2/L3 teams, and DRE lead, are pivotal for effective management.

Chapter Summary/Key Takeaways: The effective management and democratization of knowledge expedite issue resolution, mitigate human errors, prevent SLA breaches, and enhance customer satisfaction. Rigorous change management processes ensure production reliability and instill confidence in end-users.

Furthermore, clear product documentation streamlines services, reducing troubleshooting times.

In the forthcoming chapter, we will explore technological solutions aimed at establishing data observability, enhancing data governance, ensuring reliable performance, and implementing FinOps practices for data management.

Chapter Five
DRE - Technology

This chapter is pivotal to the success of the DRE strategy and its implementations. Within this chapter, we will delve into the technical projects and programs necessary to establish observability, manage production performance, governance, and FinOps. Here, we aim to facilitate the ideation of automated monitoring and self-healing solutions tailored to your data solution. I endeavor to maintain the content of this chapter as generic as possible; depending on the cloud provider, whether it be Azure, AWS, or GCP, you can design your own solutions using the available tech stacks.

The real magic begins here, where input is required from all natural team members, including L1/L2/L3 support, Solution Architects, Project Managers, and the product/development team, in addition to input from the product owner. The DRE lead will consolidate all the inputs into several stories, achievable project milestones, and segregate the duties to design, kick off, and deliver improvement programs and projects. These initiatives should be approved and funded by portfolio managers/business stakeholders. Hence, selling ideas to the leadership team becomes a significant task for the DRE lead. The DRE needs to present the benefit or ROI for each project and take complete accountability for the outcome.

Observability

1. **Monitoring** –
    a. Application layer – BI solution (pipelines, code, report performance).
    b. Platform layer – hosting platform/cloud provider (DWH/DB health).
2. **Alerts** – real time alert on failure of any components, automated ticketing system.

In a typical scenario where cloud providers offer a Platform as a Service (PaaS) deployment model, they assume responsibility for ensuring the availability of the platform, network, and clusters or virtual machines (VMs). Nevertheless, the support for applications developed atop this platform falls within the purview of the DRE team. Additionally, the DRE team is tasked with establishing robust governance mechanisms to manage expenditure on platform and infrastructure. In the event of platform unavailability, users should engage the service provider by raising a ticket for assistance. Conversely, when the platform is operational, it is imperative to monitor expenditure closely without compromising production performance. Effective platform monitoring is pivotal for optimizing production costs. Further elucidation on this topic will be provided in subsequent pages.

When undertaking any initiative within the framework of the DRE methodology, the primary focus of the DRE lead should revolve around the developmental and operational costs associated with the solution. Each program or project within this framework should demonstrate quantifiable Return on Investment (ROI).

Monitoring Application Layer – pipelines

Regardless of the specific cloud service utilized, the prevailing architectural framework employed in contemporary data organizations is predominantly the medallion architecture. Furthermore, pipelines serve as the lifeline to the entire Business Intelligence (BI) solution. Vigilantly monitoring these pipelines can unveil underlying issues pertaining to data quality or inconsistencies within integrated systems.

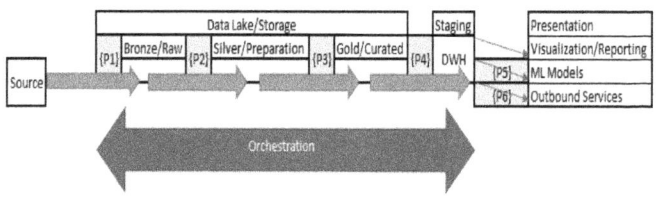

Where let's consider P1, P2, P3, P4, P5 and P6 are depicting set of pipelines: {Pn}

{P1}: Fetches data from source to Bronze/RAW layer.

{P2}: Orchestrates data from Bronze/RAW to Silver/Preparation.

{P3}: Orchestrates data from Silver/Preparation to Gold/Curated.

{P4}: Orchestrates data from Gold/Curated to Data Warehouse.

{P5}: Orchestrates data from DWH to ML Models.

{P6}: Orchestrates data from DWH to SFTP/Outbound services.

In a complex Business Intelligence (BI) solution, it is common to have over 1000 pipelines. However, attempting to monitor all of these pipelines simultaneously inevitably incurs a significant operational cost. Therefore, it is imperative to establish a strategic approach for setting up pipeline monitoring. Please adhere to the following steps outlined for devising an effective monitoring strategy and solution:

1. Please generate a comprehensive list of master pipelines wherein the failure of any child pipeline will result in the failure of the master pipeline as well. This presupposes that the pipeline sequences are structured to execute "on-success" of the preceding one, rather than solely upon "on-completion." In this context, it is imperative to consult with the product team and the data architect. Following discussions with these stakeholders, the list should be meticulously crafted. It's important to emphasize that this list adheres to the Pareto Principle, commonly known as the 80-20 rule, wherein controlling 20% of the factors ensures the reliability of the remaining 80%. The list should encompass all pertinent master pipelines, delineating the overarching data flow within the bespoke Business Intelligence (BI) solution.

2. To create an alert rule in the cloud provider's administrative portal, utilize the built-in monitoring services and alert engines offered by all cloud providers. Configure the alert specifically for instances of pipeline failure.

   a. In Phase 1, the task entails designing the alert system to dispatch emails to designated distribution lists or support analysts.

   b. In Phase 2, the task involves configuring event management software to generate automated tickets within the organization's ticketing tool, triggered by webhook or email alerts.

How to Handle Alerts: Analyze the alert thoroughly to identify the root cause. While the initial error message may suggest a data quality issue, the actual solution might extend beyond that. Observing pipeline failures or successes can point towards issues with data quality, necessitating alterations to transformation logic, or even a simple adjustment of character limits at the column level in the Data Warehouse (DWH) layer. This determination varies depending on which set of pipelines failed, denoted as {Pn}: {P1, P2,..., Pn}.

Outcomes:

1. **Swift Identification of Issues:** This allows for prompt notification of the correct team, leading to faster resolutions.

2. **Detection of Data Quality Issues:** For instance, issues with data schema are often unearthed between the silver and gold layers within the data lake.

Alternatively, these issues may arise during the data pipeline's ingestion from the curation layer to the DWH. Such alerts can trigger initiatives aimed at enhancing data quality at the source, such as drafting new agreements with data providers regarding Data Quality (DQ) metrics.

3. **Identification of Necessary Logic Changes:** Monitoring pipelines can signal the requirement for alterations in transformation logic. For example, suppose the expected length of a customer's payment method code was one character, but due to changes on the business side, more than nine payment methods are now available to customers. If a customer selects the 10th or subsequent payment method, an error may occur during the ingestion of curated data into the DWH, as the configured character limit is set to one. Depending on business requirements, either filtering out excess payment methods or adjusting the DWH column may be necessary.

Monitoring Application Layer – Data Quality

Gartner research has revealed that organizations are facing significant losses amounting to $15 million annually due to poor data quality. Shockingly, nearly 60% of these organizations do not even measure the financial toll of subpar data quality on a yearly basis, as indicated by the Gartner survey. An article from MIT cites a survey that estimates the detrimental impact of bad data to be between 15% to 25% of revenue for most companies. Additionally, it highlights that employees squander approximately 50% of their time dealing with mundane data quality tasks. Experian further corroborates these findings by reporting that companies worldwide perceive 26% of their data to be tainted, exacerbating their financial losses.

In essence, mishandling data quality issues, whether through reactive approaches or neglect, leads to losses not only in terms of monetary value but also in time and resources expended. To delve deeper into this critical issue, we will examine various types of data quality issues and discuss the essential metrics necessary for enhancing observability in this domain. The following page will feature a fishbone diagram, providing a visual summary of the ramifications of poor data quality...

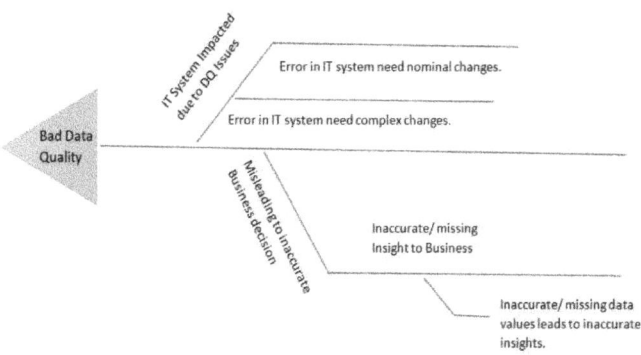

Consistency:

Suppose that during the process of transferring end-user transaction data from the point-of-sale system (source) to the Data Warehouse (target), instances of record leakage and data level leakage were identified within the target system. Specifically, it was observed that certain data records failed to load into the target system. For instance, the complete record corresponding to transaction ID "123515562" is present in the source system but is absent in the target system.

Transaction ID	Amount	Currency	Quantity
783515562	30	USD	4
123515562	100	AED	21
533519058	4	EUR	1
432517377	160	INR	3

Transaction ID	Amount	Currency	Quantity
783515562	30	USD	4
533519058	4	EUR	1
432517377	160	INR	3

Source System → Target System

Strategy: In this case the strategy to remediate is to set up a monitoring system by which we can monitor the record differences between source and target system so that it can reconcile source vs target record count anomalies.

Action: We can have automated scripts in ingestion data pipelines {P1}, by which it can measure the records differences after data load and alert us for the records count mismatch (if any). Upon those measurement we can re-run those data pipelines or have an automated solution by which it can run the prerequisite action(s) before the data reload and re-run the pipelines automatically.

Accuracy:

Accuracy in data across all domains measures the extent to which the data accurately reflect real-world entities, events, or agreed-upon sources. For instance, if the reported daily sales quantity exceeds the total available units recorded at a point-of-sale.

Strategy and Action:

Addressing this issue extends beyond the scope of Business Intelligence (BI) alone. Therefore, establishing robust collaboration with data provider teams responsible for extracting data from Point of Sale (PoS) devices is essential for addressing such use cases effectively. Drafting a comprehensive contract with the data sourcing team can facilitate this process. There's no one-size-fits-all solution; resolution depends on organizational policies and the level of collaboration among different teams.

Completeness:

Determining completeness is a nuanced task and should not be confused with correctness. It necessitates a thorough analysis to identify essential tables and columns where completeness is crucial for informed decision-making and creating business value. For example, in handling card or retail data, the significance of completeness cannot be overstated. Customer data must be sufficiently complete to enable targeted marketing of new products or devising retention strategies. Oftentimes, during manual data entry, crucial information such as email addresses or phone numbers may be overlooked unless they are explicitly marked as mandatory fields on the form. Empty columns, especially those integral to transformation logic, can cause pipeline failures, promptly notifying the support team for resolution. However, even non-essential fields like contact information, while not used for joining purposes, can significantly impact dashboards' effectiveness if left empty.

Transaction ID	Amount	Currency	Quantitity	Phone
783515562	30	USD	4	NULL
123515562	100	AED	21	NULL
533519058	4	EUR	1	NULL
432517377	160	INR	3	NULL

Strategy: In the event of missing data such as contact information, an effective approach is to modify the data entry form by implementing clear labeling and integrating JavaScript validation to ensure completeness. Additionally, if crucial data is absent from significant columns, appropriate measures are outlined in the subsequent action plan.

Action: Automated scripts can be implemented at various stages, including at, mid, or adjacent to Bronze and Silver - {P1:P2}, to systematically identify missing data points. Depending on the outcome of the validation pipeline, email alerts or triggers can be configured accordingly. Subsequently, it is imperative to communicate with data providers and request them to resend the incomplete data.

Validity (Value and Volume):

Data value validity is compromised when data fails to adhere to a specified format or business specification agreed upon during the design/requirement gathering phase. For instance, consider attributes such as currency amount, which are anticipated to be $30; however, if provided as "Thirty Dollar" or $30.00, this would constitute a breach of validity. Such discrepancies can be monitored through pipeline monitoring between the Gold and Data Warehouse (DWH) levels. The DWH will reject the ingestion of data if the format does not align with the table design specifications.

Transaction ID	Amount	Currency	Quantitity
783515562	Thirty Dollar	USD	4
123515562	100	AED	21
533519058	4	EUR	1
432517377	160	INR	3

Data volume validation is imperative when dealing with outbound services post data staging in the DWH layer. Anticipating potential user complaints about insufficient data volume or deviations from the norm, it becomes essential to conduct thorough validation.

Strategy and Action: While monitoring pipelines aids in promptly identifying anomalies, rectifying these issues exceeds the scope of a bespoke BI solution's DRE team. Extensive collaboration with the data source team is indispensable. Adhering to best practices, BI solutions ideally maintain the integrity of data received from the source. Thus, resolution necessitates dialogue and cooperation with the source team, sometimes requiring a regression to engage data value owners and business stakeholders to rectify issues at the data's origin. The DRE team can offer assistance in implementing checks at this stage. Furthermore, monitoring DQ metrics entails holding the data source team accountable, especially in cases of third-party vendor-driven operations. The DRE lead must collaborate with internal contract management, product owners, and data providers to establish agreements that address and minimize such issues at the source.

Nonetheless, volume validation remains feasible at BI-layers. Collaborating with stakeholders to determine the threshold volume or leveraging historical data spanning at least five years in the DWH, a forecasting solution employing linear regression aids in independently setting threshold volumes. It is crucial not to overlook seasonal variations when forecasting data volume.

Uniqueness:

In order to mitigate the publication of duplicate data, a specific metric has been devised. Duplicate data poses a recurring challenge during the ingestion process, often stemming from pipeline reruns due to human or system errors. For instance, a momentary network drop may cause a pipeline failure. When the pipeline is re-executed, neglecting to adhere to the knowledge base article outlined in the previous chapter may lead to the ingestion of duplicate data.

Strategy and Action:

A standard method for managing data duplication involves establishing a landing zone table, subsequently transferring distinct records to staging tables, and finally truncating the landing zone table. At times, employing a temporary table as a landing zone can be advantageous, as it will be automatically deleted upon completion of the load into the staging layer via stored procedures, triggers, or similar solutions. For expansive data warehouses, implementing periodic data cleansing proves to be an effective approach for identifying and eliminating duplicate records. Alternatively, straightforward SQL scripts can be orchestrated within a batch process flow in the data warehouse, executed after loading the main table, to remove any duplicates. However, when dealing with extensive data sizes, there exists a tradeoff regarding the removal of duplicates from the final staging layer. In such cases, it is preferable to address the issue at the ingestion stage. Subsequently, with reference to this latest data quality concern, attention will be directed towards monitoring the platform layer, exploring data warehouse health monitoring, and visual layer performance metrics in the subsequent section.

The Monitoring Platform Layer – Data Warehouse (DWH) – is a crucial area within our system. Once the processes of ingestion and transformation are completed, curated data resides in this layer. Despite ensuring data quality before its entry into this layer and maintaining 100% pipeline success, the performance of the reporting layer may still suffer if the DWH is not managed effectively as a platform. It is imperative to monitor various key performance indicators (KPIs) outlined below to ensure the smooth functioning of the DWH. Based on the Service Level Objectives (SLO) of the DWH, it's essential to establish thresholds for these KPIs. These thresholds can then be integrated into event management software to trigger automatic alerts for designated support teams.

The following KPIs are crucial for monitoring:

1. **Queued Queries:** This indicates the number of queries waiting to start executing, aggregated as a sum.

2. **DWU Limit:** Represents the service level objective of the data warehouse, aggregated as average, minimum, and maximum values.

3. **DWU Percentage:** The maximum value between CPU percentage and Data IO percentage, aggregated as average, minimum, and maximum.

4. **DWU Used:** Calculated as DWU limit multiplied by DWU percentage, aggregated as average, minimum, and maximum.

5. **Cache Hit Percentage:** Calculated as (cache hits / (cache hits + cache miss)) * 100, where cache hits are the sum of all columnstore segments hits in the local SSD cache, and cache miss is the columnstore segments misses in the local SSD cache summed across all nodes. Aggregated as average, minimum, and maximum.

6. **Cache Used Percentage:** Calculated as (cache used / cache capacity) * 100, where cache used is the sum of all bytes in the local SSD cache across all nodes, and cache capacity is the sum of the storage capacity of the local SSD cache across all nodes. Aggregated as average, minimum, and maximum.

7. **Local Tempdb Percentage:** Indicates local tempdb utilization across all compute nodes, with values emitted every five minutes, aggregated as average, minimum, and maximum.

It's worth noting that these KPIs are generic to any DWH, whether it's Microsoft, Amazon, or Google services. Additionally, certain health KPIs should be periodically audited to improve lower-level design specifications. During audits, a range of options/values may be received as output. Hence, to facilitate decision-making, pass/fail criteria will be mentioned. The larger categorization of audit assessments includes:

1. **Query Patterns**

Singleton inserts:

In a distributed system, the most efficient method for inserting large numbers of rows into a table is to execute the insertion in sizable batches. This approach ensures optimal insertion speed and enhances the quality of columnstore segments post-insertion. The purpose of this test is to identify instances where a large number of inserts correspond to a minimal row count, typically one or a very few. Enhancing these queries will accelerate the insertion process and alleviate the overall system load. The fail criterion is met when singleton inserts exceed 100 insert statements; however, it is considered best practice to have no singleton inserts. Any number falling between these thresholds warrants a warning.

Large broadcasts:

Dedicated SQL Pools employ various methods for data movement between nodes and distributions, depending on query requirements and data size. Broadcast moves entail storing the results of a query step in a replicated table within tempdb to resolve distribution incompatibility. Since a replicated table is involved, broadcast moves are typically employed when dealing with small data sizes. As data size increases, shuffle moves become more efficient. This test aims to identify cases where the query plan does not opt for the most efficient move operator, particularly focusing on large broadcast moves. Although this test is based on row count, which is just one component of size, it offers a straightforward metric for evaluating query plans. Broadcasts processing over 500 million rows or multiple broadcasts falling within the failed range are considered failures, while those between 100 million and 500 million rows fall within the warning range.

Longest Running Queries:

Due to the variable execution times of queries in dedicated SQL pools, understanding the reasons behind prolonged query execution is crucial. Factors such as inaccurate statistics, extensive data movements, under-allocation of query resources, and costly use of inline functions can contribute to prolonged query runtimes. This test captures queries with the longest execution times, with the objective of identifying the query type and data movement method. Ideally, insight into these aspects aids in optimizing query performance.

Union vs. Union ALL Usage:

The key distinction between UNION and UNION ALL lies in their handling of duplicates, with UNION removing duplicates and UNION ALL retaining them. However, duplicate removal in UNION necessitates data sorting, which can incur significant costs in terms of data movement and CPU usage. When assessing query performance, it's essential to determine whether deduplication is necessary, thereby informing the choice between UNION and UNION ALL. Queries should ideally complete within 10 minutes; exceeding this timeframe warrants a warning, prompting a review of business specifications and Service Level Objectives (SLO) to determine the optimal query design.

ResultSet Cache Hit:

Unique queries do not benefit from ResultSet cache, as queries utilizing non-deterministic functions fail to hit the ResultSet cache. Consequently, if unique queries lead to a ResultSet cache miss, it constitutes an audit failure.

2. Data Health

This section requires you to gather data from the Data Warehouse (DWH).

Ordered Column Store Usage:

When users query a columnstore table in a dedicated SQL pool, the optimizer assesses the minimum and maximum values stored in each segment. Segments falling outside the query predicate's bounds are not read from disk to memory, potentially enhancing query performance. By creating an ordered Columnstore Clustered Index (CCI), data is sorted in memory before compression, reducing segment overlapping and improving query efficiency. Meeting or exceeding the creation of 10 tables with ordered column store is considered a successful pass.

Check Trim_reason_desc for rowgroups:

The Trim Reason identifies why Compressed Row Groups (RGs) are smaller than the optimal size. Excessive smaller compressed RGs can detrimentally affect the performance of the CCI table. Failure is indicated if a significant number of tables exhibit a Trim Reason other than NO-TRIM or RESIDUAL_ROW_GROUP (table count > 10%).

Tables with High Number of Deleted Rows:

Deleted rows within Compressed RGs can impede performance by necessitating row-by-row processing. Many tables with a high count of deleted rows (table count > 10%) should be flagged as failed.

Replicated tables over 2GB:

Replicated tables, when cached, are fully stored on each node's first distribution, potentially leading to redundant storage and data movement overhead. It's advisable to keep these tables small (ideally under 2GB) to optimize storage and performance. For larger tables, hash distribution is recommended.

Healthy statistics:

Daily monitoring of key health KPIs is crucial. Self-healing solutions, such as running scripts through data orchestration services like Azure Data Factory, are recommended. Key areas to monitor include:

- ➤ Duplicate statistics
- ➤ Missing statistics
- ➤ Stale statistics
- ➤ Mismatched data types

Tables by Distribution Type:

A balanced mix of table types, including distributed, replicated, and round-robin tables, is essential to match various schema usage patterns. Monitoring for this mix ensures optimal database performance.

Tables with Small Compressed Row Groups:

Small, compressed RGs can be inefficient. Monitoring and addressing tables with a high count of smaller compressed RGs (> 10%) is necessary for optimal performance.

Data Skew Over 10%:

Data skew in hash-distributed tables can negatively impact query performance. Tables with skew over 10% should be investigated and mitigated.

Monitoring various aspects of the DWH environment is critical for maintaining optimal performance and addressing issues proactively. Metrics such as query blockings, CPU usage, data IO, memory usage, active queries, DWU utilization, cache efficiency, and deadlocks offer insights into system health and performance, enabling timely interventions and optimizations for a stable and responsive data warehouse environment..

So far we learned how to manage data observability, governance, platform performance with technical solutions. Last but not the least, look for your organization approved event monitoring application, which could be configured with monitoring solutions, to raise service tickets automatically. This hyper automation will help to get the support team flagged about the issues quickly. In next section we will explore how to track and manage the FinOps.

FinOps

FinOps in data organization involves several key steps to effectively manage the costs associated with data storage, processing, and analysis while maximizing the value derived from data. Moving to the cloud changes how you handle money for technology. Cloud services have a different way of charging you. It can be hard to manage because the costs change a lot, but it also lets you control exactly how much you spend. FinOps is a new way of managing money in the cloud. It's not just about finance people - it involves everyone who uses cloud services. FinOps makes sure everyone knows how much they're spending and what they're spending it on. It also changes how teams work together and how costs are split between them.

FinOps is all about making sure the whole organization gets the most out of their cloud services. It's not just about saving money, but also about using the cloud in the best way for the business. So, it's not just about numbers, it's about how people work together to make the most of what the cloud offers.

The cloud offers a flexible way to spend money. Instead of paying a lot upfront for computer stuff, like servers, you can pay as you go. This means you only pay for what you use, and you can change how much you use whenever you need to. It's like renting a car—you only pay for the time you use it.

Switching to this flexible way of spending money makes everyone responsible for how much they spend on the cloud. It also gives them the power to control and optimize their spending. Before, companies had to plan years ahead and spend a lot at once. Now, they can adjust their spending easily. But this new way of spending money can be tricky for finance people. They're used to knowing exactly how much everything costs. Now, they have to adapt to this new system where costs can change quickly.

That's where FinOps comes in. FinOps helps companies manage their spending in the cloud. It gives teams the tools they need to track their spending and make sure they're getting the best value for their money. But to make FinOps work, everyone in the company needs to be involved. From the engineers who use the cloud services to the finance people who track the spending, everyone needs to understand how it all works. And it's not just about saving money—it's also about making smart decisions that help the business grow. This means balancing things like performance, availability, and cost. And it means working together as a team, instead of making decisions in isolation. At its core, FinOps is a cultural practice. It's the way for teams to manage their cloud costs, where everyone takes ownership of their cloud usage supported by a central federation.

Mastering the cloud isn't just about technology or business; it's a complex challenge involving people, processes, and technology. This impacts the whole organization's culture. FinOps, which stands for Financial Operations, aims to optimize cloud spending. However, decisions must consider the "Iron Triangle" of cost, quality, and time. Balancing these factors is crucial. The company must prioritize speed (time to market), quality (performance, reliability, availability), and cost to achieve success.

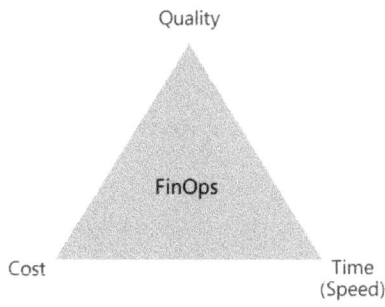

The aim of FinOps isn't solely about cutting costs but creating the most value. Therefore, trade-offs are necessary. By aligning actions with these principles, companies can maximize the benefits of cloud technology while controlling expenses. It's about finding the right balance to drive efficiency and innovation. In essence, mastering the cloud isn't just about adopting new tools; it's about reshaping how organizations operate and adapt in the digital era.

Key milestones for building a FinOps culture of collaboration

Crawl	Walk	Run
Engineers are still learning what FinOps is and their role within it.	Engineers understand the importance of FinOps within the business.	Engineers consider financial impact during each lifecycle.
FinOps metrics are available to teams, but engineers don't actively use the metrics.	Teams monitor and optimize this metric.	Engineers actively look for FinOps opportunities. Engineers proactively confirm budget and highlight changes that will impact costs.
Finance and engineers are only just starting to meet.	Engineering and Finance are aware of each other and understand what motivators drive each other.	FinOps team advocates with Engineering teams for investment for solid financial endeavors.

FinOps Maturity Model by FinOps Foundation

Key milestones for cloud business decision-making

Crawl	Walk	Run
Establish a simple hierarchy of decision-making authority and accountability.	Decision and accountability structure and processes are well documented.	Standardized FinOps decision making processes are in place, utilizing agreed FinOps metrics.
Define efficiency metrics that support business improvements.	Mature product teams have implemented unit economics and can use them to tell effective cost management stories.	Unit costs for key services are developed and tracked over time for efficiency.
Users are tracking costs at the account level but are not using unit economics to measure their cost effectiveness.	KPIs are developed to measure the cost effectiveness of desired business outcomes.	Business and product owners understand that their design decisions drive cost.
FinOps metrics are available to teams but there is no set ritual followed by engineers around the metrics.	Leadership makes decisions based on the cost impact and business value.	Able to make proactive and predictive decisions based on business goals.

Key milestones for accurate and timely reporting

Crawl	Walk	Run
Match granularity of cost and usage data on incoming source files, though reporting separately.	Ingest data from multiple data sources, normalizing cost metrics.	Consistent data lake of usage, cost, performance, utilization data; sharing with other disciplines across the org.
Ensure metadata being applied to hierarchy and resources is consistent across cloud providers and data sources.	Ability to create consistent reports for different clouds, possibly using different reports.	Ability to run a single report with multiple clouds.

"Teams need to collaborate very closely to find the best balance between all objectives to support the one single objective that really matters: Business value." – Dirk Brinkman, Principal Cloud Solutions Architect, Microsoft

The FinOps Foundation suggests some important things to help manage costs better:

1. **Analyze Trends:** Look at how costs change over time and compare them within your team. This can show where you're doing well or where there might be problems.

2. **Define Unit Economics:** Understand the costs of your cloud services in detail, both technically and from a business perspective. This helps in making smart decisions.

3. **Report Effectively:** Build a strong system for reporting costs so that you can understand where the value lies and where improvements can be made.

4. **Compare with Others:** See how your costs compare to others in your industry. This can give insights into what challenges you might face and how to overcome them.

Here's a summarized structured approach:

People

1. **Define Clear Objectives:** Begin by defining clear objectives for your FinOps strategy within the data organization. Understand what you aim to achieve—whether it's cost optimization, better resource allocation, or improving ROI on data-related investments.

2. **Establish Governance:** Develop governance policies and guidelines for managing data-related costs. This includes defining roles and responsibilities, establishing approval processes for resource allocation, and implementing cost tracking mechanisms.

3. **Training and Awareness:** Provide training and awareness programs to educate teams about FinOps principles, cost management best practices, and the importance of responsible resource usage. Ensuring that teams are knowledgeable about cost implications helps in fostering a culture of cost-consciousness and accountability.

4. **Collaboration and Communication:** Foster collaboration between finance, IT, and data teams to align financial goals with technical objectives. Effective communication and collaboration facilitate better decision-making, resource planning, and problem-solving, leading to improved financial outcomes for the data organization.

Process

1. Cost Allocation and Accountability: Implement mechanisms to allocate data-related costs accurately across different teams, projects, or departments. This ensures accountability and transparency in cost management and encourages responsible resource usage.

2. Implement Budgeting and Forecasting: Establish budgets for data-related expenses and develop forecasting models to predict future costs based on usage trends and growth projections. Budgeting and forecasting help in planning and managing expenses effectively, avoiding cost overruns, and ensuring financial sustainability

3. Continuous Improvement: Continuously evaluate and refine your FinOps practices based on feedback, performance metrics, and evolving business needs. Regularly review cost optimization strategies, identify areas for improvement, and implement changes to optimize costs further and enhance the value derived from data.

Technology

1. **Cost Visibility and Monitoring:** Use tools and platforms to monitor and track data-related costs in real-time. This includes monitoring storage usage, data processing costs, and expenses related to data analytics tools and services. Having visibility into costs enables proactive decision-making and cost optimization.

2. **Optimization Strategies:** Develop optimization strategies to reduce unnecessary costs and maximize the efficiency of data-related processes. This may involve optimizing storage usage, leveraging cost-effective storage options (e.g., tiered storage), rightsizing infrastructure resources, and optimizing data processing workflows.

3. **Automate Cost Management:** Utilize automation tools and scripts to automate routine cost management tasks such as cost monitoring, resource provisioning, and cost optimization. Automation helps in reducing manual effort, improving accuracy, and ensuring timely responses to cost-related issues.

FinOps in the light of DRE

FinOps is important for the whole company, but since this book is about Data Reliability Engineering (DRE), let's talk about how we can combine FinOps strategies with DRE practices to create a reliable and affordable system for managing data. If you're interested in learning more about FinOps, you can visit The FinOps Foundation website for detailed information. It's essential to understand the framework and figure out how it can fit well with your specific situation. By doing this, you can ensure that you're making the most of your resources while keeping your data reliable and cost-effective.

As the DRE lead, your responsibilities begin with breaking down the architecture. A good place to start is by defining short-term and long-term goals. Long-term goals can be planned based on information about FinOps, but for immediate benefits, it's best to take a practical approach to optimize current costs. Short-term goals will allow you to understand and promote the best practices right away.

Breaking down the architecture means understanding how different parts of a system work together. It's like dismantling a machine to see each piece. We need to delve deeper than data reliability for BI- layers, focusing on cloud infrastructure components. Understanding allows setting goals for improvement.

Long-term goals are plans for the future. They might include reducing costs over time, improving efficiency, or making the system more reliable. These goals can be based on information about FinOps, which is a set of practices for managing financial resources in cloud computing.

But while long-term goals are important, it's also essential to focus on immediate benefits. That's where short-term goals come in. These goals are smaller and more achievable in the short term. They might involve finding ways to save money right away or implementing best practices that can have an immediate impact.

By setting both short-term and long-term goals, you can work towards improving the architecture while also realizing immediate benefits. This approach allows you to make progress quickly while also planning for the future. And by evangelizing these best practices, you can encourage others to join you in improving the system.

Apart from following below mentioned strategies, continuously monitor and review cloud costs, identifying further optimization opportunities. Regularly optimize configurations, workflows, and resources to align with evolving business needs and budget constraints. Defining right SLO with Product Owner gives right direction. For example, if PO mentions, expected load time for a report is 90 sec, and you are already less than that, do not invest to improve it further, rather try to maintain the same availability.

To optimize cloud costs in a business intelligence solution, consider these steps:

1. **Data Usage Analysis:** Understand data usage patterns to identify unnecessary data extraction. Remove redundant or infrequently accessed data.

2. **Scheduled Extracts:** Schedule data extraction during off-peak hours to benefit from lower cloud service rates.

3. **Compression and Encryption:** Implement data compression and encryption techniques to reduce storage and transfer costs.

4. **Query Optimization:** Optimize queries to minimize data extraction volumes and processing time, thus reducing costs.

5. **Resource Scaling:** Utilize auto-scaling features to adjust resources dynamically based on demand, preventing over-provisioning.

6. **Data Filtering:** Apply filters to extract only relevant data, reducing the volume of data transferred and stored.

7. **Data Retention Policies:** Implement policies for data retention to manage storage costs efficiently. Delete outdated or unused data regularly.

8. **Monitoring and Alerts:** Set up monitoring tools to track resource usage and cost trends. Receive alerts for any unexpected spikes or deviations.

9. **Cost Allocation:** Allocate costs accurately across departments or projects to optimize resource utilization and budget allocation.

10. **Evaluate Service Tiers:** Assess different service tiers offered by cloud providers and choose the most cost-effective option that meets your extraction requirements.

11. **Implement Cost Monitoring and Alerts:** Set up cost monitoring tools and alerts to track spending in real-time. Identify cost spikes or inefficiencies promptly and take corrective actions

12. **Explore Reserved Instances or Savings Plans:** Commit to reserved instances (AWS) or savings plans (Azure) for predictable workloads to benefit

from significant cost savings compared to on-demand pricing.

13. **Use Spot Instances or Preemptible VMs:** Consider using spot instances or preemptible VMs for non-critical or fault-tolerant transformation tasks to take advantage of discounted pricing.

14. **Explore Reserved Instances or Savings Plans:** Commit to reserved instances (AWS) or savings plans (Azure) for predictable workloads to benefit from significant cost savings compared to on-demand pricing.

Now, let's talk about what we can do right away. For the long-term goal, it's up to you to choose your strategy based on the framework designed by the FinOps Foundation. I don't want to limit you because your organization's budget and future plans are unique, so you need to figure out what works best for you. Still, there are some good practices that, if you follow them, can help you save money right now. After that, focus on developing your team, improving your processes, and using technology like automation and AI to make these savings last. It's all about finding a solution that works for you in the long run.

Data Warehouse:

1. **Choose the Right Storage Option:** Decide which storage option is best for your data warehouse. This could be hot storage for frequently accessed data and cold storage for less frequently accessed data. Hot

storage is more expensive but faster, while cold storage is cheaper but slower.

2. **Data Compression:** Use compression techniques to reduce the amount of storage space needed for your data. This can help lower storage costs without sacrificing performance.

3. **Partitioning and Indexing:** Partition your data based on how it's accessed and create indexes for frequently queried columns. This can improve query performance and reduce costs by minimizing the amount of data that needs to be processed.

4. **Data Archiving and Cleanup:** Regularly archive or delete old, unused data to free up storage space and reduce costs. This ensures that you're only paying for the storage you actually need.

5. **Optimize Query Performance:** Write efficient queries that minimize the amount of data scanned and processed. This can help reduce the cost of running queries by using fewer resources.

6. **Monitor and Adjust:** Continuously monitor your data warehouse usage and costs and make adjustments as needed. This could involve scaling up or down based on demand or optimizing resource allocation to reduce costs.

7. **Use Cost Management Tools:** Take advantage of cost management tools provided by your cloud provider to track spending, set budgets, and identify opportunities for cost savings.

ETL overall:

1. **Optimize Cluster Size:** Adjust the size of your Databricks clusters based on your workload. Use smaller clusters during low-demand periods and scale up when needed.

2. **Auto-scaling:** Enable auto-scaling to automatically adjust the number of nodes in your cluster based on workload. This ensures you're only paying for resources when you need them.

3. **Instance Types:** Choose the most cost-effective instance types for your workloads. Consider using preemptible or spot instances for non-critical tasks to save money. This is discounted rentals for computing power. They're cheaper because they can be taken away if someone else needs them urgently. So, they're good for tasks that can handle interruptions or aren't super important.

4. **Idle Resource Termination:** Set up automatic termination for idle clusters or instances to avoid paying for unused resources.

5. **Storage Optimization:** Optimize storage by compressing data and using efficient file formats to reduce storage costs.

6. **Data Lifecycle Management:** Implement data lifecycle policies to automatically delete or archive data that is no longer needed, reducing storage costs.

7. **Monitoring and Optimization:** Regularly monitor resource usage and performance to identify opportunities for further optimization.

Storage accounts:

1. **Understand Your Data:** First, understand what kind of data you're storing and how frequently you need to access it. Some data may be accessed frequently, while other data may be accessed infrequently or even rarely.

2. **Choose the Right Storage Class:** Most cloud providers offer different storage classes tailored to different needs. For data you access frequently, use a standard storage class. For data you access less often, consider using a cheaper storage class designed for infrequent access.

3. **Utilize Lifecycle Policies:** Set up lifecycle policies to automatically move or delete data based on its age or other criteria. This ensures that you're not paying for storage of data that you no longer need.

4. **Compress and Encrypt Data:** Compressing data before storing it can help reduce storage costs, as compressed data takes up less space. Additionally, encrypting data before storing it can protect it while also helping you avoid any additional charges for encryption services.

5. **Monitor and Adjust:** Regularly monitor your storage usage and costs and adjust your storage strategy as needed. If you notice that certain data is not being accessed as frequently as you expected, consider moving it to a cheaper storage class or deleting it altogether.

Please note, strategy to optimize the cost on production environment will differ in many dimensions compared to NPE (Non-production environment). It depends on what the business needs.

For example, in the production environments, we might need to make a lot of things very quickly, focus on SLO, and decide the resource allocation wisely. But in NPEs, places where we're just testing or developing stuff, we might be able to live with fewer resources with lower configuration.

Epilogue/Conclusion

I trust that the book thus far has been thought-provoking for all of you. Data Reliability Engineering (DRE) is a multifaceted topic, necessitating careful consideration when implementing a DRE strategy. Therefore, it is crucial to focus on delineating the scope of your program to mitigate confusion down the line, particularly within large matrix organizations. It is advisable to refer to the shared responsibility matrix established within your organization for guidance.

Here are some key steps to consider:

1. Define the scope of DRE, which typically encompasses activities from the ingestion layer to the reporting layer. However, it may extend beyond these boundaries to include additional layers.

2. Collaborate closely with business stakeholders to define Service Level Objectives (SLOs). Align your efforts with these objectives to effectively manage costs during DRE implementation.

3. Educate end users and super users. Sometimes, a simple workshop or discussion is all that is needed to ensure optimal performance in production environments.

4. Enhance observability. Monitoring and measuring are essential components of control. Without proper observability, you cannot effectively manage or mitigate issues.

5. Work closely with solution architects to define a sustainable solution delivery roadmap. This collaboration ensures that DRE initiatives align with broader organizational objectives.

6. Assemble a team of passionate technologists and establish robust processes around them. A dedicated team with the right expertise is crucial for successful DRE implementation.

Bibliography

- https://community.hitachivantara.com/blogs/subramanian-v/2023/09/15/a-guide-to-data-reliability-engineering
- https://www.databricks.com/glossary/medallion-architecture
- https://docs.microsoft.com/en-us/azure/architecture/data-guide/big-data/
- https://www.montecarlodata.com/blog-data-ingestion/
- https://learn.microsoft.com/en-us/azure/synapse-analytics/sql-data-warehouse/sql-data-warehouse-manage-monitor
- https://learn.microsoft.com/en-us/azure/synapse-analytics/sql-data-warehouse/sql-data-warehouse-concept-resource-utilization-query-activity
- https://cloud.google.com/bigquery/docs/query-queues#:~:text=You%20can%20monitor%20the%20query,jobs%20in%20a%20pending%20state
- https://docs.aws.amazon.com/redshift/latest/dg/cm-c-wlm-query-monitoring-rules.html

- https://learn.microsoft.com/en-us/azure/synapse-analytics/sql-data-warehouse/sql-data-warehouse-manage-monitor
- https://docs.moogsoft.com/Enterprise.8.0.0/en/servicenow-management.html
- https://learn.microsoft.com/en-us/azure/well-architected/services/storage/storage-accounts/security
- https://learn.microsoft.com/en-us/azure/storage/blobs/security-recommendations
- https://www.youtube.com/watch?v=2SLZiOR3f6c
- https://www.youtube.com/watch?v=X6cmJ2IbVzo
- https://www.geeksforgeeks.org/data-warehousing-security/
- https://www.tutorialspoint.com/dwh/dwh_security.htm
- https://www.finops.org/

Acknowledgement

I extend my sincere gratitude to my esteemed colleagues, Shritosh and Subrata, for their invaluable support in our engineering endeavors. Shritosh's adept guidance in structuring FinOps deployment and enhancing Data Warehouse reliability has been instrumental. Similarly, Subrata's pivotal role in defining KPIs for data quality and substantial contributions to the FinOps domain of this publication are commendable. Their unwavering dedication and collaborative spirit have been pivotal in transforming ideas into tangible realities. Moreover, their efforts in facilitating post-deployment monitoring of benefits before documenting in this research paper turned book are deeply appreciated. Their contributions have significantly enriched this endeavor.

Shritosh Khairnar, a seasoned Site Reliability Engineer, holds a Master's in Computer Application. With over 12 years of expertise, he has excelled in roles spanning Database Architect, Administrator, and Developer across diverse sectors including Energy, BFSI, Health, Shipping, and Engineering. Outside work, he indulges in socializing with friends, playing cricket or snooker, and unwinding with quality films. He resides with his wife, daughter, mother, and father, cherishing family time amidst professional pursuits. With a rich blend of technical acumen and personal interests, Shritosh navigates both his professional and personal spheres with adeptness and fulfillment.

LinkedIn - https://www.linkedin.com/in/shritosh-khairnar-64248916b

Email - Khairnar.shritosh4@gmail.com

Subrata Bera, a seasoned professional in Information Technology, boasts a Master's degree in Computer Application from Siliguri Institute of Technology, West Bengal, complemented by a Bachelor's degree from Sikkim Manipal University. With over 8+ years of IT expertise. Proficient in Cloud Services (Azure, AWS), SQL, Databricks, Data Warehousing, ETL, Python programming, and Power BI, Subrata's journey is adorned with accolades for his invaluable contributions. His ethos centers on problem-solving and continuous learning. Beyond work, Subrata indulges in art, literature, and Football. Hailing from West Bengal, he resides in Bangalore while his parents remain in their hometown.

LinkedIn - https://www.linkedin.com/in/subrata-bera/

Email - subratabera33@yahoo.com

www.ingramcontent.com/pod-product-compliance
Lightning Source LLC
LaVergne TN
LVHW061345080526
838199LV00094B/7378